REPORT

OF REMARKS BY REV. G. W. PERKINS,

ON MR. STUART'S BOOK

"CONSCIENCE AND THE CONSTITUTION,"

AT A MEETING IN GUILFORD, AUGUST 1, 1850. COMMEMORATIVE OF EMANCIPATION IN THE WEST INDIES.

There is a point of degradation to which even the Slave rarely descends. There are few Slaves who are *willing to be Slaves.* Slavery can affect much in debasing the human character. Indeed its worst crime is its power and will to deface the image of God in its victims. Now and then it works out the most difficult problem in this its work of human degradation, and ultimately succeeds in so thoroughly crushing, and brutalizing the soul, that the wretched being is willing to be a Slave. But this is rare. Nearly all Slaves long to be free. When they have lost that desire, they have reached the last and lowest stage of debasement, *save one.*

In this low deep there is one still lower: it is the condition of a mind *willing to be a slave-catcher*. That position, voluntarily taken, implies such a combination of selfishness, subserviency, profligacy, and utter destitution of all noble human qualities, that we stand aghast at the sight of one who can thus make of himself such a moral monster. But many of our public men at Washington have seemed emulous to plunge, each deeper than the other, into this debasing subserviency. Of these, none has showed more willingness to harness himself into the car of slavery, and do its dirtiest work than DANIEL WEBSTER: when of his own motion, he bowed low his neck, and cheerfully offered to support "to the fullest extent" that monstrous bill of abominations for recapturing refugees from bondage.

But I recal one part of my position. There is a lower deep still. It is the condition of that man who voluntarily comes forward to *defend the slave-catcher*, and brings his Bible to prove that it is a work of justice and a sacred duty to be slave-catchers. Beyond this the soul of man would seem to be incapable of going. To this last stage, has come, REV. MOSES STUART, in his book entitled, "Conscience and the Constitution."

This book I propose at the present time to examine. Not that it requires any great labor, or has thoughts of any great value. Indeed with so much *innocency* has the author crossed his own track, that perhaps the best criticism which could be constructed, would be the simple process, of placing in parallel columns, his own contradictory assertions. But as he has probably given us those views which interest and sway the public mind, it may be well to bestow on them a little attention. In so doing, I shall be compelled to follow to some extent the topics by him discussed. If I should allude to some positions too plain to need refutation, remember that the *name* of Mr. Stuart may give currency to sentiments, which have no sound argument to sustain them.

ALLEGED ABRAHAMIC SLAVERY.

Mr. Stuart commences with the stale argument that Abraham was a slave holder. "Abraham's family of *slaves* must have consisted of at least 1590 persons." It is not easy to see the relevancy of this fact somewhat ostentatiously put forth, to the matter in debate. For one who alleges that Abraham was a slave holder must be held to the strict proof of the three following propositions, before his argument can have the slightest weight in apology for Mr. Webster.

(*a*) That Abrahamic Slavery was the *same thing* as American Slavery.

(*b*) That Abraham taught or practiced, the duty of catching refugee slaves.

(*c*) That Abraham's example in the matter, imposes the slightest obligation on us to do likewise.

If he fails to prove either of these positions, his argument is of no value. For the question is not whether there existed in old times various kinds of *servitude:* and that there was in the family of Abraham a certain class of persons called *servants.* That is conceded. But the point to be proved is, that the condition of Abraham's servants was that of *American Slavery.* American slavery as defined by the atrocious laws of the slave states is this. "Slaves shall be deemed, sold, taken and reputed to be *chattels personal* in the hands of their owners, and possessors, their executors, administrators and assigns, *to all intents, constructions, and purposes whatsoever.*" "The slave is one who is in the power of a master to whom he belongs. The master may sell him, dispose of his person, his industry and his labor: *he can do nothing, possess nothing, nor acquire any thing* but what must belong to his master."

Mr. Stuart must prove that Abraham's *servants*, were *such* servants: held under similar law: or he proves nothing to the purpose. But that he has not attempted. There is not the shadow of such proof in the Bible. Nay, there is most ample evidence to the contrary. For remember that Abraham and his wife were old people — that they wandered about among other wandering tribes, with no higher human government to enforce the subjection of their slaves. It is most plainly absurd that one old man and woman in *such circumstances* could *hold* as *chattels personal*, 1590 human beings, many of them well armed! Indeed Mr. Stuart with the characteristic incoherency of reasoning which habit gives to some men, and *opium* to others, subsequently acknowledges that "what the Arabian Sheikhs *now* are to their petty tribes, Abraham was to his 1590 servants"! This he coolly states, after he had argued that Abraham was a slave holder! If Abraham was simply a *Sheikh* and *not* a slaveholder, his case has nothing to do with our argument. Again, did Abraham catch fugitives from oppression? Did he teach the duty? Mr. Stuart does not allege this.

But allowing that Abrahamic slavery *was* identical with American slavery: what then? What do Mr. Stuart and the whole tribe of apologists for slavery mean, when they continually thrust forward Abraham as a slave holder? Do they mean that Abraham's conduct either justifies, or renders any less criminal, our like conduct? If they say "no," then all they say about Abraham is a mere piece of argumentative impertinence: it has nothing to do with the question. If they say "yes," then hold them to that point, and do not let them escape from it. Compel them to stand firmly to the position that *what Abraham did, it is right for us to do.* Abraham lied: Abraham had concubines: Abraham was a poligamist. Then it is right for us to do likewise. If the slave holder can screen himself under Abraham's example, so may the liar and the fornicator, and bigamist. If any of you ever hear Abraham's example quoted as an extenuation of slavery, push home this logical demonstration upon such an opponent, and let him not escape. Compel him to abide by his own principles. He is not to be allowed to do as Mr. Stuart has done, who after he had quoted Abraham and used him in defence of Mr. Webster, blindly concedes that Abraham was *not* a slave holder at all: and that "*not* what the patriarchs did, is our rule."

ALLEGED HEBREW SLAVERY.

Mr. Stuart next argues with equal logic from the alleged fact of *slavery among the Hebrews, sanctioned by their divine system of laws.* But here also, his whole diffuse argument can be met with this simple question. "Mr. Stuart do you mean to assert that slavery among the Hebrews was *identical with*, or like unto, American slavery defined and enforced by South Carolina law? Do you maintain that the Hebrews, had God's permission to reduce human beings to chattels personal, to all intents, constructions and purposes whatsoever? that God allowed them to buy and sell human beings like brutes? to put them up at auction with cattle and sheep? that the tribe of Dan had a divine law authorising them to *breed slaves* for the shambles of the tribe of Judah? that Jerusalem was a regular slave market? Do you assert that *such* slavery existed among the Hebrews? If Mr. Stuart says, "no," then ask him: "what do you allege the example of Hebrew slavery, for? We are arguing about *American slavery:* a well known thing or institution, defined by law which *does* allow all these atrocities. If Hebrew slavery is *not* like that, it has nothing to do with the question. Your whole elaborate dissertation is just as much out of place as it would be, if the people of America should deliberate whether they should send back the Hungarian refugees to be hung, and Mr. Stuart in arguing the affirmative should prove that the Austrian government did right in hanging murderers!"

If Mr. Stuart takes the other side of the alternative, and declares that Hebrew servitude *was* like American slaves, then we call on him to prove it. It is not enough to quote a few texts about "bondmen," to show that there was a *species* of servitude among the Hebrews. No one denies that. But he must prove the *identity of Hebrew slavery with American slavery.* That he has not attempted. He well knows it cannot be done. Nay he has virtually acknowledged that they were not alike. What a piece of logical impertinence then is his argument.

But for the sake of argument we will allow more than Mr. Stuart claims: we will concede that Hebrew slavery *was* identical with American slavery, as defined by the savage code of South Carolina: and that *God explicitly commanded* the Hebrews to form and maintain such a system. But what then? What does even that prove? Does it prove that what the Jews did, and did by God's permission, *we* are authorized to do? If one says "no"—then what is the argument about. If the example of the Jews does *not* justify us, then all talk about that example, in our present discussion, is mere rant and dust. Why allege that example for justification, if it affords no justification?

But if the reply be, "yes;" it is as right for *us* to hold slaves as for the Jew, then we hold you to that position; and you shall not fly from it. See what the Jews did; and were *commanded by God* to do. Turn to Deut. 7: 1, 2. "When the Lord thy God shall deliver them [Canaanites] before thee, thou shalt smite them and *utterly destroy them:* thou shalt make no covenant with them, nor *shew mercy to them.*" *That*, the Jews to some extent did, and

God commanded it. They were to *exterminate* the nations: to kill men, women and children!

Here then hold your opponent to his principles. If he alleges the Jew as example and justification; then he must maintain that a war of extermination is right now: that our troops in Mexico might have butchered men, women and children in their march and have exterminated the people. "The devil can quote Scripture for his purposes," and our regimental chaplains could have justified the butchery from Scripture, as logically as slavery is defended from the example of the Jews.

Even *if* Hebrew slavery was the same atrocious system as ours, no argument can be constructed from it, in defence of American slavery, which would not involve conclusions, which even a savage would reject. I shall here enter into no argument to show what Hebrew servitude really was: it would occupy too much time.

HEBREW LAW FAVORABLE TO FREEDOM.

But in the course of his argument from Hebrew servitude, Mr. Stuart meets with some passages, which give him no small trouble. In Leviticus 25: 10, we read, "Ye shall hallow the fiftieth year, and *proclaim liberty*, throughout all the land *unto all the inhabitants thereof*." That looks very anti-slavery: If we could get such an article inserted into the Constitution of South Carolina, we should know what it meant. We presume the slave holders would know so well what it meant, that they would be quite likely to vote against it.

But true to those instincts which lead a certain class of interpreters to give a passage of the Bible which *seems* to lean towards Slavery, the most wide unqualified sweep of meaning, and to put every passage which seems to favor liberty into cramping irons and torture out of it all its meaning, Mr. Stewart finds but a partial act of emancipation in this explicit verse. He says that this law of freedom was intended to apply *only* to the *Hebrews*, who were slaves: *not* to the *heathen* who were slaves *among* the Hebrews.

But this interpretation is impossible, for the Hebrews were *not* slaves. It is expressly and repeatedly declared that the Hebrews were to be "*as hired* SERVANTS"—*not* bondmen. If liberty was to be given, it was surely to be given to those in bondage. The *heathen* were to be held as *bondmen*, the Hebrew, only as a *hired servant*, by his brother Hebrew. If liberty was to be given to *all* the inhabitants, then surely it must apply specially and most certainly to those who are deprived of liberty. If a broad and sweeping law should now be passed by Congress, giving liberty to *all the inhabitants of the District of Columbia:* and if a man should say that the law *meant only the apprentices* of the District, *not* the slaves, he would be as wise an interpreter of human law, as Mr. Stuart of the laws of Moses.

Mr. Stuart quotes another passage in which it is said that the "heathen shall be your bond men for ever"—of course he argues that they could not have been set free at the end of fifty years.—We are then brought to this position, that there is a seeming, or real contradiction between different enactments. For my present purpose it is not necessary to decide whether the discrepancy be apparent or real. The same rule of interpretation will hold, and will apply equally to both human and divine law. In case of actual or apparent conflict of laws, that interpretation is to prevail, and that law is to be made supreme, which is most on the side of right, justice and liberty. If God has made a law which gives liberty to every bondman at the end of fifty years: this is evidently a just and human law: plainly designed to make still lighter, the comparatively light servitude—*not slavery*—which alone God sanctioned. That must stand. If we find a law, which *seems* to be in conflict with it: which *seems* to be harsh or cruel—then the soberest rules of judicial interpretation requires us either to give the harsh law a milder interpretation, or to cut the knot by actually carrying out the just law to the practical abrogation of the harsh one. As it is plainly absurd that *all* should be free, and *some* held in perpetual bondage; we are to understand that all are to be free, and *none* are to be held in perpetual bondage.

This must be our conclusion, even *if* God had in one passage *commanded* servants to be set free at the end of every fifty years; and in another passage expressly *allowed* the Hebrew to retain his bondman forever. But there is no such conflict of laws. The text "they shall be your bondman forever," is simply analogous to such phrases as these:—"The North will supply dough-faces forever. The meaning is not that *each individual dough-face* is *always* or forever used. On the contrary the South only use one as long as may be necessary: and from time to time dismiss one set for a fresh supply. But the idea is, that the South can *always* find such a set of men, when they want them.

So when the Jew wanted bondmen he was *always* to go to the heathen for them: he was only to treat his brother Hebrew as a *hired servant.* The heathen world, was *always* to be their source of supply. Yet even this bondage was carefully guarded by the provision, that *each individual bondman*, alive at the year of jubilee, was to be emancipated.

GUARANTEES OF HEBREW LAW TO THE FUGITIVE.

There is another formidable abolition passage, which must be removed out of the way. In Deut. 23: 15, 16, it is said, "Thou shalt not deliver unto his master the servant which is escaped from his master unto thee: he shall dwell with thee even among you in that place which he shall choose." That looks hard towards emancipation, and does not seem to teach slave-catching theology. If such a provision had been inserted into the Constitution of the United States, instead of the famous article about "delivering up"—"those held to service"—I doubt whether it would have been misunderstood, either North or South: whether even Mr. Webster could have found in such a clause, foundation for that atrocious bill, which he is now pledged to sustain. But Mr. Stuart thinks that our Constitution *does* require fugitives from oppression to be given up: and as the divine Constitution expressly *forbids* the fugitive to be given up—the divine law must be put on to the bed of Procrastes, and racked till it will protect the slave catcher. Mr. Stewart *says*, this divine law did *not* mean to protect all, but *only* a small class of fugitives: that if a fugitive slave from Gad, took refuge down in Manasseh he *was* to be delivered up: [He has most singularly forgotten to tell us where this important law is to be found; a law so much to his purpose it was very necessary to produce.] But if a slave escaped from Moab, or a heathen country, and fled to Judea; *such* a fugitive was not to be given up. So the law meant! Thus must the Bible when it speaks in favor of liberty, have all the life crushed out of it.

Will Mr. Stuart be so kind as to tell us, when God has said he did *not* mean that the law should apply to *all* fugitives. Strange to say, the reason why he thinks this provision *could not* apply to all fugitives, is this:—*if fugitives had such rights, it would make slavery insecure!* Indeed: If God had put some merciful laws into his code, slave property would be less secure and valuable:—therefore God did not put in such laws; and those which *seem* to be so merciful to the bondman, must be tortured out of all their meaning.

On the contrary how evident is it, that God designed by these two celebrated enactments relative to the year of jubilee, and the recapture of fugitives, to *make light*, even a light and modified form of servitude—they are plainly inserted in God's constitution, for the very purpose of *rendering insecure*, and *bringing to an end*, even that modification of bondage which he temporarily allowed: the very design is to secure kind treatment, and effectually cut up abuses, which so naturally grow up around any form of bondage. By an obviously righteous rule of interpretation, they are to have the fullest meaning the words will bear. But the necessities of American slavery and American politicians are imperious, and the word of God must justify their course.

MR. STUART'S PITY.

When Mr. Stuart has thus proved that it is a Christian duty to send back fugitives, from a passage which *forbade* the Jews to do that thing; he seems to be affected even by his own conclusion. He says "*we pity* the restored fugitive and have reason enough to pity him when he is sent back to be delivered into the hands of enraged cruelty." Yes indeed: who does not know that the recaptured fugitive is made to feel all the ingenious and fiendlike cruelty which a revengeful slave-holder can inflict? that the poor wretch is with horrible emphasis "made an example of?" that tortures by the whip, the paddle, the gag, the chain, are made to eat into his flesh like fire? that he dies a slow death under the infliction, or is sold to one of those two fates, which the slave has learned to dread more than death—the rice-planter—or that modified form of diabolism, "the *slave-breaker*." To such a fearful doom is the fugitive sent back. Mr. Stuart "pities" him.

Perhaps you will expect then that Mr. Stuart would find something in the Bible, or in the human heart to excuse us from the revolting act of dooming a fellow being to such a fate. But his iron theology cannot bend: and he adds "the responsibility, however, for bad treatment of the slave [thus sent back] rests not in the least degree on us of the North!"

His reasoning cannot fail to remind one of the analogous argument of one of Milton's characters. Satan after his fall, enters into "a compact" with his fellows, to go in search of the new world, whereof some news had reached hell; with the design of winning its happy inmates to sin. He finds paradise, and for a time stands gazing on the beauty of its scenery, and the bliss of its sinless residents. Even the devil relents, as he thinks of the horrors to which he was to tempt them—and is half persuaded that he would not do so foul a deed, but at length concludes,

"Should I, at your harmless innocence
Melt, *as I do.* [the devil actually "felt pity"]
Yet public reason just
. . . . *compels* me now
To do, what else, though damned, I should abhor."

Of equal worth is the "pity" and the "public reasons" of those who send back the unhappy refugee to sufferings which are not exceeded except in hell. Satan could plead "a compact," as well as politicians.

ABOLITIONISM IN THE PROPHETS.

Mr. Stuart passes on to the *prophets;* and in their writings finds some very troublesome passages. For he seems particularly afflicted, and calls out his whole army of hermenentic apparatus, when he comes in sight of a verse which seems to be severe on slavery.—There are such passages as these; "*Let the oppressed go free.*"—

"*Break every yoke.*" "Wo unto him that buildeth his house by unrighteousness: that useth his neighbour's service without wages, and giveth him not for his work." "*Hide the outcasts; betray not him that wandereth.*" Similar passages are numerous. They teach abolitionism. They speak the heartiest and most incendiary language of rebuke to the slaveholder.

Mr. Stuart's mode of evading these passages is very peculiar, and evidently smacks of that interview with the "great expounder" whom "I have seen not long since for a few moments." His argument is: God gave the Jews a *constitution*: that constitution allowed Slavery: the prophets came to *enforce* that constitution: they had no power to alter it: therefore what they said must not be interpreted as disallowing Slavery.

The logic is certainly compact. But let us examine it a little.

"That Constitution allowed Slavery." That it allowed anything like American Slavery we utterly deny. That there was a modified form of servitude allowed, so hedged in by laws as to secure its termination, is conceded. But Hebrew servitude has hardly any more resemblance to American Slavery, than the Pope's reign of terror at Rome is like the present government of Connecticut.—*Both are Governments:* there the resemblance ends. So American slaves and Hebrew bondmen, are both called *servants:* but their respective conditions and rights were totally unlike. We protest therefore against this constantly repeated fallacy wrapped up in the words "Hebrew Slavery."

But further: *if* Hebrew slavery *was* like American slavery, we contend that the prophets had as much power to abrogate it, as Moses had to establish it. God spoke by Moses: God spoke by the prophets. Whatever power Moses had, that same power the prophets had. Whatever power God had to establish an institution; surely God had the same power to abolish it. Most certainly *if* God had established such an institution as American slavery, we should expect that he would send other messengers to abolish it. If God solemnly commands men to "let the oppressed go free"—it is a most curious mode of argument to assert that God allowed the Jews *once* to oppress the heathen; therefore he *cannot* mean that that oppression must cease now: and therefore the command to let the oppressed go free *must mean* that they *are not* to go free. Mr. Stuart's whole mode of reasoning is precisely like that of our politicians in Congress, and which he probably learned of Mr. Webster. These politicians take for granted that the great object of the United States Constitution was to perpetuate and guarantee slavery; and on that assumption torture and wrench all its other provisions to compel them to agree with this supreme end: and would make every law and measure, to subserve the same purpose. So Mr. Stuart seems to think that Slavery was the chief end of the Mosaic code. Its securities for freedom are explained away; and the express declarations of the prophets, strong and clear for freedom, must be made to countenance the lawfulness and perpetuity of slavery.—I reject such assumptions.

If we find a command in the prophets which requires the emancipation of the slaves—for what less can be the meaning of the words, "Let the oppressed go free"—then it is to be interpreted just as any similar act of human government would be. If S. Carolina *now* should pass a law that all *the oppressed should be free*, that law would be in force, whatever might have been her previous laws.

But Mr. Stuart has another curious mode of reading the anti-slavery texts of the Bible. The prophet had said "Wo to him that useth his neighbours without wages, and giveth him not for his work." Nothing could more accurately describe the practice of all slaveholders. The language is quite as harsh as that of the "ultras" whom Mr. Stuart hates so cordially. But he cannot allow that so respectable a man as a Slaveholder could be spoken of so pointedly. So he goes mousing after some other interpretation; and finds that in the context there is mention made of one Shallum who was rather slack in paying his laborers, and finds that the prophet was reproving *him*, and did not mean slaveholders at all!

For "nobody ever heard that *slaves* should have wages." therefore the prophet *did not mean that it was wrong to keep wages from them!* Truly a second Daniel come to interpret. Because a wicked act is very common, therefore the prophet did not mean to condemn it! Because slaveholders, all the world over, with the true characteristic meanness of the *tribe*, never do pay wages to their laborers, therefore the prophet did not mean them, when he solemnly, and in the name of God, *cursed* those who refuse to pay wages!!

Mr. Stewart with characteristic *innocency*, fails to see that this mode of interpretation is not only ridiculous, but is suicidal to his own position. For *if* this prophetic denunciation must be limited to Shallum, because Shallum is mentioned in the context, then the same rule must be applied elsewhere. When Paul commanded servants to be obedient, he *only meant those servants in Corinth or Colosse*, to whom he was writing: he did *not* mean American slaves: when he advised Onesimus to return to Philemon, he *only* meant Onesimus, he did not mean that American slaves, should even be advised to return.

One plain supposition will put the whole Old Testament argument in its true light Just let us suppose the following provisions incorporated into the Constitution of S. Carolina: "No slave shall be compelled to return to his master: he may emigrate and live where he chooses:" "at the end of every 50 years, whatever servitude has survived so long shall cease; *every man* shall be free"—" from henceforth every yoke shall be broken: all the oppressed shall be free—and every man shall be cursed who will not pay wages to the man who works for him." How long would slavery continue in that State? It would take the ingenuity of Calhoun, Webster and Stuart united to make out the sanction of slavery from *such* a constitution. Yet such was the Jewish constitution; which our learned professor would bend down to the support of the slave-holder.

THE NEW TESTAMENT.

Mr. Stuart next appeals to the New Testament. His arguments and interpretations in this department are equally remarkable. He commences with a long and elaborate argument to show that *Christ did not intermeddle in political affairs:* very well, that is all true, as it is common place. But what then? What is the fact so ostentatiously paraded for? Does Mr. Stuart mean to argue, that because Christ had nothing to do with politics, therefore Christians *now* must have nothing to do with politics? that because Christ did not vote, therefore we Christians must not vote? that because Christ did not oppose, expose, and aim to repeal, bad laws, therefore Christians now, must not do it? Is that his meaning? Plainly not. Then why this pompous array of Christ's example in this particular if we are not to imitate it?—what argumentative impertinence to allege the example of Christ in *not* intermeddling with politics, when all admit, that Christians now *are* to have much to do with polities, and *ought*, to vote and act in political affairs.

Suppose Christ did not intermeddle with slavery: what then? He did not intermeddle with *adultery*. There was a case brought before him: a clear case: there was no denial of the fact: no extenuating circumstance. He would have nothing to do with it: nay, expressly said to the adultress, "neither do I condemn thee." But what does it prove? that *we* are to have nothing to do with condemning adultery: or with making laws for its suppression? Certainly, if there is any force in Mr. Stuart's appeal to the example of Christ, about slavery.

The force of the argument will appear stronger, if we suppose that a *slave-holder* had been brought before Christ, instead of the adultress. Suppose Christ had said to the *slave-holder*, "neither do I condemn thee." It would have been quoted as the sufficient and triumphant demonstration, in all ages, that *we* had no right to condemn the slave-holder. All these modes of argument prove the desperate attempts of a certain class of writers, to find or make something out of the Bible which shall extenuate slave-holding, or minister to their own dislike of anti-slavery men.—Modes of argument which would be scouted as intolerable and dishonest when applied to any other subject, are gravely put forth by men who ought to be great, in apologies for slavery.

THE APOSTLES.

Mr. Stuart next quotes a variety of passages from the epistles, which I have not room to insert. It is not necessary, for the import of them is the same, and I concede freely all they teach.—There are quite a number of texts which speak of the duties of *servants*. These are all quoted at length in the book before us, as if they had something to do with the argument. But here again, the question comes up: what do such passages prove? why, they prove that the slave *does* have certain duties to perform! That's all. But who denies or doubts that? such proofs have nothing at all to do with the question, whether those masters had any *rights* over them as slaves? The question relates to the right and wrong of American slavery; and our duty to aid the refugee from oppression.

Suppose I should find myself on board a pirate ship, and find there a number of captives, forced out of their own homes and compelled to remain and work in that pirate ship. I converse with them and console them with Christian hopes and truths. I also advise them to perform their work well on board the pirate ship: not to steal—not to return evil for evil even if the pirates abuse them: but to glorify God before the pirates by industry and good behavior. Some friend of the pirates hears this advice, and uses it to show that I approve, or at least *allow* piracy. He comforts the pirates, who occasionally have misgivings as to the righteousness of their calling by repeating to them my exhortation to the prisoner. "Observe," he says, "that your prisoners are exhorted to behave well; to discharge their duties to you: he does not exhort them to rebel or fight. It is plain therefore that you are engaged in a business which no one ought to intermeddle with!"

That is precisely the logic of Mr. Stuart's argument from the Apostolic addresses to servants. His whole argument proceeds on the assumption, that because a man is under obligation to perform certain duties in certain relations, therefore the relation itself is right. Whereas the obligation to such duties, proves nothing as to the rightfulness of the relation. The prisoner in a pirate ship has certain duties to perform, *while there:* but that proves nothing as to his right to escape from that pirate ship, *if he can.* The man who is struck, owes certain duties to the man who struck him: he is to forgive him, pray for him, and turn the other cheek, [that is, not resist.] But that by no means proves that he should not get out of the striker's way and reach, *if he can.* The slave owes certain duties to his master *while in that relation*, but that proves nothing as to the master's right over him, nor as to his own right to escape, *if he can.*

The pompous show of Apostolic directions to servants paraded in all pro-slavery publications, proves that *servants owe certain duties* to their masters—and nothing more.

But while Mr. Stuart with the true instincts of a Southern slave-holder, gives such a broad and comprehensive sweep to directions to *slaves*, he is very careful to put into his cramping irons the texts addressed to the *masters.* The spirit of freedom in them must be carefully squeezed out by the full force of hermeneutic screws. Thus Paul (Col. 4: 1) commands "masters to give unto their servants [slaves] *justice and equity*," as Mr. Stuart translates it. This does not look pro-slavery. If *we* were slaves, we should think that *justice* and *equity*, did *not* consist in forcing us to work without wages: in *holding* us by *means of wicked laws* in a condition in which we could be bought and sold like brutes: in *compelling* us to remain in a state in which it was a *crime* to read, or teach our children to read: in leaving us at death to be divided up like cattle among heirs. It is singular *justice* and *equity*, to *force* a fellow being to remain in a state, "where the mass of slaves *must* live in a virtual concubinage:" where "as an inevitable consequence, the young females are at the mercy of their masters"—where "their eternal welfare is grieviously neglected." *We* should think, that if *God* commanded *our* masters to treat us with justice and equity, that he meant we should have a right to education, wages, and legal protection: that justice and equity consisted in the speediest possible emancipation from such a horrible condition: that it is impossible to treat a slave with justice and equity, and yet keep him as a slave.

But Mr. Stuart's interpretation of the passage can only be equalled by his "Shallum argument." The substance of it is this—"the Apostle meant that slaves should *continue* to be slaves; *should be* held in a condition which *is* unjust and unequal, therefore justice and equity to *them* could not mean that *they* should be taken out of that condition." He says "all excessive and rigorous demands are forbidden by this passage and *nothing more*, is meant by it." We should like to know if Mr. Stuart would consider *himself* treated with *justice* and *equity*, if *held as a slave*, though not compelled to work very hard.

But the interpretation of 1 Cor. 7: 20—24 is so curious, that I must quote the passage; putting in the word *slave* as Mr. Stuart contends it should be translated.

"Let every man abide in the same calling wherein he was called. Art thou called being a servant? [*slave*] care not for it; but if thou mayest be made free, use it rather. For he that is called in the Lord, being a servant, [*slave*] is the Lord's freeman: likewise also he that is called, being free, is Christ's servant, [*slave.*]

Ye are bought with a price; be not ye the servants [slaves] of men."

With a cold sneer he says; it means that slaves "*are not to make a fuss*:" "are forbidden to be fractious and querulous and *uneasy*, MERELY because they are in bondage." Indeed: "*merely because they are in bondage!* We wish the men who can speak thus lightly of the most revolting condition to which a human being could be reduced, could have a taste of the cup. For *one week*, we should like to see the "great expounder" and his "Boswell," put into the slave gang, and worked in a rice field. If they did not feel "uneasy" and "make a fuss," we should then say, let them remain slaves, till they did become "uneasy."

He then falls back on his grammar. He says, the Greek word, *kresai*, here translated *use it*, is, in the original left without an accusative case; so that it would read, "if thou canst become free, use .... rather." The question then arises, how is the ellipsis to be filled up? He says that "many commentators" here insert the word, *douleia*, slavery; so that it would read "if thou canst become free use [prefer, choose] slavery rather!!" The Apostle is represented as actually advising them to continue slaves, even when they could be free. Mr. Stuart himself says of this interpretation, "it is certainly the most facile philology." (page 53.)

But this is rather too much even for his capacious digestion: and he "on the whole *thinks*" that freedom, not slavery, should fill up the ellipsis Most wonderful conclusion—*on the whole, thinks* Paul recommended freedom, rather than slavery.

The common sense meaning of the passage is this: Art thou called, being a slave: care not for it:" i. e. bear it with a Christian spirit. "But if thou *canst become* free [the true translation] use it, rather." "*Canst become:*" the Apostle does not put on any limitation. *Interpreters*, put in qualifications: "if thou canst *with the consent of your master*, then choose it." The Apostle leaves the slave with this bold, and freedom loving exhortation: "if thou *canst* be free, secure freedom."

He then proceeds to assign a reason why he should not be a slave. The converted slave, is "the Lord's freeman." But the Christian slave cannot perform many duties which a Christian ought to do: he *cannot educate his children*, as a Christian ought; he *cannot educate himself nor read God's word*, as a Christian ought; he *cannot put his children to such trades and employments as may* be for their good, as a Christian ought; he *cannot protect the chastity of his wife and daughter*, as a Christian ought; he cannot gain time and money for the promotion of Christ's cause, as a Christian ought; as a "chattel personal" he is owned like property, as a Christian ought *not* to be. Therefore there are good reasons why, if he *can* be free, *he ought to get free:* and the Apostle advises him so to do. "Ye are *bought with a price*, be NOT the slaves of men"—that is, "Christ has bought you with his blood, and made you Christians: and as Christians demand of you certain duties, which the condition of slavery forbids, therefore *be not slaves*, but freemen, IF YOU CAN." This is the noble sentiment of a noble hearted man, and of a freedom loving Bible. But the Bible in the hands of such interpreters as Mr. Stuart is like Sampson, blinded and chained, and then harnessed into the car of sin and slavery, and made to do the base work of the slave catcher.

DUTY OF SLAVE CATCHING.

Mr. Stuart having thus prepared the way, approaches the main topic; the question of the recapture of fugitives from oppression. The main Scriptural battery, he finds in the case of Onesimus and Philemon. *Paul, he says, sent back a fugitive slave.* On this fact, he charges those who refuse to do the same as having a "conscience" like "Dominic," "James 2—Jeffriess," "the Hindoo mother," "hangers of witches," and "naked Quakers," and works himself up into a phrenzy.

What a miserable fallacy, in this appeal to the case of Onesimus. Did Paul *arrest* Onesimus? Did he deliver him over to slave catchers and brutal agents? slave catchers who put irons on him and dragged him off while Onesimus begged Paul to keep him from these terrible human blood hounds? Did he see him lodged safely in jail to be *forced* back to Philemon? knowing that when his master got him back, there awaited him that terrible apparatus for "breaking down a runaway," which the ingenuity of a Southern overseer can devise? Did Paul do this and then pharasaically wipe his mouth and say: "I am not responsible, for Philemon's bad treatment of Onesimus?" If you say, *no*, then what do you allege this case for? If Paul did *not* do, what you want us to do, why talk about Paul.

But, such outrages that bill of abominations which Mr. Webster pledged himself to support "*to the fullest extent*," requires us to do, or allow to be done. What utter perversion of the Scriptures then to quote Paul's example: how strange that men can repeat the stale falsehood that "Paul sent back a fugitive slave: for *in our legal meaning* of the term, *he did no such thing.*

The utmost that Paul did, was *to advise* Onesimus to return to Philemon: or at the furthest, *urge it on him as a duty*, to return. Now this we are perfectly willing that Mr. Stuart, and all slave catchers in heart should do. We will not oppose them in the least. On the contrary we advise them to do it. We should like much that Mr. Stuart, now that he is dismissed from his professorship, should go down to Boston where he will find a great host of refugees, and find them out and urge them to go back. He may read to them the epistle to Philemon: he may argue, entreat, advise, and labor with them. If they consent to go, he may write letters to their masters. He may get Mr. Webster on his next visit to Boston to aid in this labor of love, and they both may use their great minds in this noble work. We think the employment would be a very suitable one for both of them. The refugees, I have no doubt, would listen to them with profound attention: and we would not put a straw in the way of the return of any slave, whom they could induce to go. "If any *can* be free and use slavery rather," we cannot help it. These two gentlemen have certainly put themselves into a position near akin to servitude: Let them persuade the slave back then, *if they can.*

But Paul did not even *advise* Onesimus, to return *as a slave.* For in language the most terse and explicit possible he tells Philemon that he was sent back, "NOT as a slave" [servant.] Yet in the teeth of Paul's own positive denial, we are told that, Paul *did* send back a fugitive slave. *If* Philemon afterwards used Onesimus as a slave; he did what Paul forbade him to do; and what consequently it was a sin for him to do: and we are here inquiring what Paul did. Paul only used *moral influence* to induce Onesimus to return; and he was to return NOT to the condition of a slave. How can that justify us in *forcing back* a fugitive in irons, to the *most horrid forms of perpetual slavery?* What a mind that must be, which can thus get

"A license from the Holy Book
For brutal lust and hell's red wrong.
Give Heaven the credit of a deed
Which shames the nether pit."

Mr. Stuart having completed his Scriptural argument, proceeds to argue the duty of recapturing and sending back fugitives from oppression, on other grounds. The gist of the whole argument is, "There has been a compact for such recapture; therefore we must do it; it is our duty to do it." Instead of following what I conceive to be his sophistry, let me state those positions which seem to me to be right; and which, if clearly seen will best meet the difficulties in men's minds. I shall state those principles which are as true in law, as in morals.

If in any law or instrument, there are real or seeming contradictions, the cases which arise under it, are to be decided in favor of right and freedom. The Constitution of the United States, was designed according to its own express statement for the very purpose of "establishing justice," and "securing the blessings of liberty to ourselves and our posterity."

This is plain:—In this great instrument I find *one clause only*, which *seems* to be at variance with the general aim of the whole instrument. It requires that "persons held to service in one state," "escaping into another, shall be delivered up." Now according to all legal rules of interpretation, that clause is to be construed *strictly* so as not to conflict with the *main design* of the document:—it is to have no more meaning and breadth, than the nature of language *compels* us to give it:—and if there was a bad meaning intended, and the language does not convey that bad meaning, then we are not to allow anything in consequence of such a mistake, even if we know it was a mistake. Shylock agreed for his *pound of flesh.* He *expected* to have the blood too. He would have inserted an agreement for the blood, if *he had thought of it:* or had supposed that any difficulty would result from the omission. But the "compact" said nothing of the blood. So he was held to a *strict* construction. He might have the pound of flesh, but was to be hung if he took a drop of blood.

Now whatever the slaveholder *meant*, he forgot to put into the compact the word slave. There is a well defined and technical condition known as slavery: it means, *in law*, one certain thing, and *nothing* else. There is the word *slave* which *in law* has one definite meaning: and no other. Now I ask where is the compact to *deliver up a slave.* There is an article about delivering up "those held to service or labor." That is another legal phrase which has its own meaning. Those to whom that legal description answers, may be given up, and no others. For in a constitution made for the *express purpose* of securing liberty, we cannot allow any interpretation which makes havoc with human liberty, unless the language *compels* us. If Shylock wanted the blood, why did he not *say so?* If the slaveholder wanted us to send back his slaves, why did he not say so? According to strict legal construction therefore, there was *not* any compact to deliver up refugee *slaves.* We deny therefore Mr. Stuart's main position.

But for the sake of argument we will allow that there was a compact to deliver up slaves, and that *we* personally made the compact:—What then is our duty?

Nothing can be plainer than that a *compact to do a wrong thing is not binding.* There is great guilt in making such a compact; and one who has made it, is in a wretched condition. But law and Gospel are both plain on the point. Herod made a compact with the daughter of Herodias. She claimed the head of John Baptist, on the ground of a "COMPACT" to give whatsoever she might ask. Now what was Herod's duty? Why according to Mr. Stuart's theology, Herod *was bound by his compact* to put John to death. For Mr. Stuart denounces in the severest terms all pretences of conscience in such a case, and sneeringly exclaims:—"Talk of Conscience, in violating a solemn compact?" If Herod had appealed to a higher law, the law of God which forbade him to commit murder, though he had made a compact to do it—Mr. Stuart would have replied: "A higher law? Who has discovered and determined such a law? the honest answer would be, their own passions and prejudices. It is a conscience wholly subjective. Talk of conscience in violating a solemn compact!" So that according to our Master in Israel, the teacher of our young ministers; no one has ever discovered and determined this *higher law of God:* and one who appeals to it, appeals to his own passions and prejudices. Herod kept his compact and murdered an innocent man: and Mr. Stuart, if consistent, must approve his conduct. Herod had begun a course of guilt and blood, and therefore he must wade on and sin the more.

Some years ago, forty men, bound themselves by a solemn "COMPACT" not to eat or drink till they had killed Paul. If one of these men with some misgivings of conscience had applied to Mr. Stuart for advice, this reverend divine must have told him, "talk of conscience in violating a solemn compact! go on and kill Paul to be sure. I shall *pity* him if he suffers much while you stab or poison him; but you are not responsible for consequences after you have made a solemn COMPACT to kill him."

Such are the legitimate results of Mr. Stuart's principles. But our common sense rejects such doctrines however artfully they may be decked with sophistry.

We return then to the case before us. God commands me to feed the hungry, and clothe the naked, and be kind to the poor.—Human law forbids me to perform these acts of humanity towards a man with a dark skin, who is fleeing from those worse than blood hounds, the slave catchers. Suppose I DID make a compact to obey law; and SUCH A LAW: What am I to do? Why, plainly, repent of my sin in making such a compact with the Devil: obey God, and perform these acts of humanity to the suffering fugitive. To send a human being to a condition, where as a fugitive he will be treated with relentless barbarity—where from him and his family, education, property, home rights and all we hold dear, will be forever withheld—is plainly contrary to God's will, if there is any such thing as love and humanity taught in the Bible. Suppose human law requires me to do these wicked acts, and I promised to obey: what is my duty? Herod-like, having dipped my arms in crime, shall I plunge all over in? No: I must repent with deep self abhorrence, violate my compact to do wrong; and do right.

These are the positions we must take, allowing to the full extent all that is said about a "COMPACT" and the nature of that compact. But I deny altogether, the slave-holder's view of that compact The Constitution of the United States, is no such compact as he and his slave catching allies would have it. That Constitution we are ready most sacredly to obey.

Let any one who OWES SERVICE be arrested: let him be arrested by "due process of law," and tried by "due process of law"—as the Constitution expressly requires.

We shall abide by all such decisions. For the Constitution is a PRO-LIBERTY compact, made *for the protection of freedom and right—perverted* by slave-holders to their own purposes.

They tell us of a compact. But what kind of compact, did we *personally* make? a compact to obey whatever laws wicked men might choose to make, and SAY were constitutional? A compact to worship the Pope if Catholics could ever get hold of the Constitution,—as slave-holders have done, and pass laws requiring from us such worship, SAYING they were constitutional? A compact to obey any laws however abominable, which ambitious and corrupt men desirous of office might be disposed to pass? Did we ever agree to do any such thing? We, as freemen, and taking the freeman's oath have sworn to "maintain the Constitution of the United States." That we shall do.

It is a plain case that a Constitution, which is right, which every good man can swear to support, and ought to support, may fall into hands base enough to pervert it; and wicked enough to pass laws at variance with it. It is a conceivable state of things that a law should be passed forbidding us as Congregationalists to meet and worship God, under a Constitution which allows freedom of conscience, and that the Courts fall in with the corruption of the times, and sustain the law and violate the Constitution. The citizen has taken an oath to OBEY the Constitution AND the law. But he is now in a position in which he CANNOT do both. He MUST violate one or the other. What must he do, VIOLATE his first and highest oath to obey the Constitution; and obey a wicked law? or sacredly *observe* his oath to the Constitution and to the right, and disregard the wicked law? In this last case he violates no oath: he never made a compact to obey whatever wicked laws might be made under a righteous Constitution.

Now that is analogous to our case under the Constitution of the United States. It is a *pro-liberty* compact; securing justice, life, liberty to all. Under it and in violation of it and of the divine law, legislators have passed wicked laws, forbidding those duties of humanity which God requires. *Some* Courts have sustained those laws. But we cannot obey the Constitution AND the law for they are in conflict. What shall we do? NOT violate the compact and oath to sustain the Constitution of the United States: but *keep our compact*, and disregard the wicked law.

Or, to put the same thought in a somewhat different form:—When there are distinct constituted authorities, and the requirements of one are at variance with those of the other, so that obedience to both is impossible, *we must obey the higher power:* and if we take an oath to obey both, we ALWAYS take it *with the implied proviso*, and understanding, that in case there shall be such conflict, now or hereafter, we shall thus obey the superior authority. So clear is this understanding, that we violate no oath in disregarding the lower authority.

Thus for instance we are bound to obey and swear to obey or sustain the Constitution of the United States *and* the Constitution of Connecticut. It is always *understood*, when we take this oath, that *if* there should be found on examination or trial, any thing in the Constitution of Connecticut, or any thing in a new State Constitution afterwards formed—or in any future laws of the State, at variance with the Constitution of the United States —then we are to obey the higher authority, and violate no oath in disobeying the authority of Connecticut. For if our oath ran thus, "We swear to obey the Constitution of Connecticut, *if* not at variance with the Constitution of the United States"—then it would be plain that we violate no compact, in disobeying the Constitution of Connecticut, when there does arise such variance. But this proviso is as *really implied*, as if actually inserted in our oath.

Now to apply the principle. There are these two rightful authorities—the Constitution of the United States *and* the law of God. We are bound to obey both: we are under a "compact" to obey both. We are not in the habit of taking oaths to obey God. We do take an oath to support the Constitution of the United States. But this oath is always taken with the *express understanding*, that in case of conflict between the authority of the United States, and the authority of God that we shall obey God, and disobey the United States. That this is so will appear evident from the following supposition. Suppose the oath ran thus: "I swear to support and obey the Constitution and laws of the United States, even if they are or shall be at variance with God's law." How many men would take such an oath? I will venture to say, not one in America: for it would be their unanimous and prompt objection, "the very thought is blasphemy; for whatever promise, oath or compact we make, it is *of course understood* with this reservation, provided, that in all this there is to be nothing required of us, at variance with the law of God." When, therefore, the authority of the United States and the law of God *do* come into conflict and we disobey the United States; so far from violating any oath or compact, we are most *sacredly observing* our oath, for we are doing the very thing which we pledged ourselves to do. *They* violate their compact, who do that which is wrong, because it may be required by the United States; for they *do* the very thing, which their very oath bound them *not* to do.

If any one says that this is dangerous doctrine, and virtually subverting all law, I reply that there are cases in which the private citizen *must* decide whether he will obey law or not. When the law is so constructed as to require or forbid personal acts, he is compelled to decide whether he will obey or not. Thus if the law forbids me to worship Christ, I *must* decide either that I will, or will not worship Christ; and must use my private judgment in the case. If I obey the law, I use my private judgment. If I disobey the law, I use my private judgment. The law advocated by Mr. Webster is of this nature. It forbids me to render the offices of humanity to a suffering and innocent refugee. The law forces me to decide whether I will obey God or man.

The position here advocated, is the one taken by martyrs and heroic reformers in all ages. The early Christians were all *law-breakers:* the Puritans were law-breakers—our Pilgrim fathers were law-breakers--our revolutionary fathers were law-breakers—Luther was a law-breaker--Knox was a law-breaker—Daniel was a law-breaker—the Apostles were law-breakers—many of our modern Missionaries are law-breakers—the men who aided the escape of Lafayette from Olmutz were law-breakers. Each and all of them, found sin framed into law, and treated it as they did any other sin.

It is unpleasant to be compelled to make these statements. For the stability of our republican institutions rests on a sacred reverence for law in the minds of the people. When that is gone, our government must rest on the same foundation with other governments; the bayonet. Most carefully are we accustomed to cherish therefore a profound respect for law. In its own sphere it *is* the law of God. But when our politicians take advantage of this New England sentiment, and having framed sin into law, come and urge on us obedience to it because it is law, and would make our conscience a pack horse for wickedness, then we must recur to the great original principles of right. We deliberately tell them, "your wicked laws we shall disobey."

What do Mr. Stuart and Mr. Webster mean, by their contemptuous rejection of "a power higher than the constitution?" What does Mr. Stuart mean, when with atheistic hardihood he says, "There is a higher law than this *they say.* But I ask; *who has discovered and determined such a law?*" Has it come to this that our leading statesmen and theologians deny the authority of God? have they in their desperate defence of slavery, wallowed down into the lowest lie of Hobbes, that "the law of the land is the supreme rule of right?" Does our professor of Biblical Literature not know that there is a God, and that we ought to obey God rather than man?

We know not what to think. A certain Senator, happened to let fall the self evident truth that there was "a power higher than the Constitution." For this sentiment he was assailed by his brother Senators, with a savage ferocity. Mr. Webster pours out a ponderous storm of hate on the sentiment and its abettors; and Mr. Stuart discharges his vials of wrath and learning too. Do they mean that we *are* to trample on God's law, if the Constitution so orders? Have they become so beside themselves, in their mad worship of party, and servile subserviency to slavery-dom, that they will blaspheme their God, and uproot the foundation of all law and right? Has Mr. Stuart so long applied the idolatrous epithet of *godlike* to Mr. Webster, that like the stupid heathen we read of, he begins to worship the god his own hands made?

Hours might be occupied in quoting the testimonies and deeds of men, who have feared God rather than man. Of the old Christians, Tertullian says, "We should be subject to magistrates and princes and powers, with all obedience, but this *within the bounds of religious duty*." The sainted Ignatius, was addressed by the emperor, "what a wicked wretch art thou, thus to endeavor to transgress our commands, and to persuade others also to do likewise." The emperor Aurelianus in a law put forth against Christians, says, "we have heard that the *laws are violated* by those who in our times call themselves Christians. Seize these people and punish them with various kinds of torture." Cyprian says, "what more glorious . . . . . than not to have obeyed human and profane laws." He was required by the pro-consul to sacrifice because "the emperor has *put forth* an edict which requires all to observe the Roman ceremonies"—but he replied: "I am a Christian; I know no God but the true God, the Creator of all things." A young Numidian Christian was arrested and put to the torture, While he was on the rack, the pro-consul said "you ought to have obeyed the imperial edict." He replied, "I now only revere the law of God." Another was arrested for *harboring runaway Christians*: and when he pleaded before the court, "I could not decline to receive my brethren," the judge sternly replied, "the imperial edict ought to have outweighed these considerations." He nobly replied, "*God is more than emperor*." Celsus, the great enemy of the Christians, declares that they deserved all the persecution they endured, "because they held assemblies contrary to law," and "would not believe and honor Gods, according to law."

But I must stop. On Mr. Stuart's principles, the heathen persecutor was right; and the Christian martyrs were a race of fanatics, acting out "their own passions" under "the pretense of conscience."

Our Missionary Societies, are law-breakers. Mr. Stevens, agent of the Am. Board, chartered a vessel to go from Canton up the coast. He landed at various places and distributed books; which to the Chinese, were "incendiary publications." "Almost every where the magistrates opposed him:" they bade him depart saying, "intercourse between foreigners and Chinese is forbidden by law." But Mr. Stevens persisted and distributed 20,000 incendiary publications.

Even our legal writers have advanced sentiments far in advance of the heathenish and servile doctrines put forth by the Andover Professor of Biblical interpretation. Blackstone says,

"The law of nature, being co-eval with mankind, and dictated by God himself, is of course superior in obligation to any other. It is binding all over the globe, in all countries, at all times. No human laws have any validity, if contrary to this; and such of them as are valid derive all their force, and all their authority mediately, or immediately from this original."

Lord Brougham says, "Tell me not of rights—of the property of the planter in his slaves. In vain you tell me of the laws which sanction such a claim. There is a law above all the enactments of human codes: it is the law written by the finger of God upon the heart of man; and by that law eternal and unchangeable, while men despise fraud, and loathe rapine and abhor blood, they shall reject with indignation the wild and guilty fantasy that man can hold property in man."

Mr. Stuart in his defense of slave-catching has been obliged to pervert the Bible, and deny the fundamental principles of all morality—he has adopted the most servile maxims of despotism, and the worst sentiments of infidelity. His doctrines would disgust all classes of men but that lowest form of humanity, the slave-catcher and the slave-dealer.

I have no doubt that even the slave-holder cordially despises the cringing spirit developed in this book: and while he likes to have his slaves brought back, regards alike the blood-hound that throttled them, and the biped that arrested them. For even the slaveholder could take a position in advance of Mr. Stuart. In the recent trial of Gen. Lopez at New Orleans, Mr. Sigur declined to give evidence and said, "If he were to go to the gallows, he would not hesitate upon this point. He submitted in all due defference to any action of the Court, but he could not give the evidence called for. He did not consider a compliance with law always the highest morality. There was a law among the ancient Romans compelling the citizens to worship certain statutes, but the Christians did not consider it the duty, or as a moral obligation, to obey this law. So he would not violate the most sacred duty of friendship and hospitality, to satisfy the demand of a hard and unjust law."

DEFENCE OF MR. WEBSTER.

After a general argument on the duty of sending back refugees from oppression; Mr. Stuart proceeds to the direct defence of Mr. Webster. Now we certainly have a right to claim from our Northern politicians, that they shall go no farther than is absolutely necessary, in yielding to the demands of slavery-dom. If they verily believe that they have made a compact, to do such vile and base work, as they speak of; they ought not to *volunteer* any special readiness in the job. They ought at least to tell their masters: "True, we have agreed to catch your slaves for you; and our conscience compels us to fulfil the contract: but we don't like it: we feel like pirates when we are doing it. We beg of you not to press the matter too far. We entreat you not to compel us to get down lower than we are."

Indeed the time was, when a politician might have been expected to have a little spirit and to have addressed his overseers in this manner:—"You have got a compact—as you say—now make the most of it. If the compact means what you say, you shall get nothing more out of us. We'll not help in any way to facilitate the savage work of slave hunting; rather than pass any new laws to help such an atrocious system, we will see the whole South, at the bottom of the sea. Take the pound of flesh if you can get it; but we'll *not give you the blood too:* nay, if you take a drop of blood, we'll hang you, as we do pirates."

Mr. Webster did not manfully meet the slave-holder: he did not even *beg off*. But when the slave-holder thought that Northern men were getting tired of acting the blood hound for them, and becoming above their business; a new and stronger lash must be put on the whip. He brought into the Senate a bill to which he added some amendments, which, to say nothing of their unconstitutionality, for cold blooded atrocity I will venture to say were never surpassed in the code of any savage people under heaven. Mr. Webster has not even the grace to keep silence; much less, to utter one manly word. With a subserviency which seems impossible in any human being in his sober senses, he *volunteers* his aid and complaisantly proclaims, "My *friend*, has a bill on the subject now before the Senate, with some amendments to it, which I *propose to support*, WITH ALL ITS PROVISIONS, TO THE FULLEST EXTENT."

Mr. Stuart must undertake the defence of such a man. But the enormity of such a bill was rather too much even for his capacious digestion. With his usual skill in hermeneutics, he must therefore compel Mr. Webster as well as the Bible, to *mean* just the opposite of what he *says*. He begins by informing us, "I always *supposed* from the first, that there *must* be some *mistake*, [in Mr. Webster's speech] which had been overlooked." True, Mr. Webster's words were taken down by accomplished reporters. Mr. Webster *revised his own speech*, before it was published. Mr. Webster, *until he began to lose popularity* never hinted at any mistake. But Mr. Stuart *supposed* there *must* be one. He did not know where to find it: but sure he was, Mr. Webster did not mean, what he said.

At length "a newspaper," we know not what, suggested that "by the *change of the location of a single word* which *probably* stands as it now does, by mistake"—the whole difficulty might be obviated. Just take the word *which*, and put it before a different clause, and Mr. Webster's declaration would read thus: ". . . a bill, *which*, with some amendments, I propose" &c. So that the idea would be that Mr. Webster only intended to support the monstrous bill, *after* amendments. But all this is plainly an after thought. The reporters are skillful; *Mr. Webster revised his own speech* for the press: no correction was thought of, till the bad effects of his speech began to come on him. Moreover the other clauses, show that Mr. Stuart's reading of the obnoxious sentence cannot be right. For if you will read the sentence as altered by Mr. Stuart, it would make Mr. Webster's declaration to be merely this: "My friend, has a bill, which, after I have *cut out some* of its main provisions, I intend to support with *all* its provisions, to the fullest extent." Mr. Webster, in his *sober* senses, never uttered such an unmeaning sentence as that. Mr. Mason had a bill, with some amendments, worse than the bill itself: the bill *and* amendments, were *both* before the Senate, when Mr. Webster spoke. What utter nonsense for him to proclaim in such emphatic terms that he meant to support *that bill in all its provisions*, to the FULLEST EXTENT, when he did *not* mean to support its *main* provisions, to *any* extent. Mr. Stuart's skill in extracting ideas from words, is wonderful. When GOD says that "liberty shall be proclaimed to all;" Mr. Stuart forces "all" to mean a *part*. When God commands that "the oppressed shall go free," Mr. Stuart interprets it as meaning that the slaves; those most oppressed; shall *not* go free. When Mr. Webster declares that he *would* support *all* the provisions; Mr. Stuart maintains that he meant that he would *not* support them. "The change of a single word," is an exceedingly convenient plan for politicians and interpreters. They can now make their speeches and the Bible work by the rule of contraries, if they will get somebody to "*suppose* they *must* have meant" as they did *not* say: and then "change only one word."

"Mr. Webster has personally assured [Mr. Stuart] that his speech was in accordance with the correction here made." But we can receive no such private, circuitous, explanations of a public speech: explanations coming too so *suspiciously late:* first suggested by an unknown newspaper; and which only end in self-contradiction.

But why vindicate Mr. Webster from the crime of supporting Mr. Mason's bill. Has not Mr. Stuart put forth an elaborate book to prove that fugitive slaves ought to be sent back? that God required it? and that Paul himself set us the example of so holy a work? Did not Mr. Stuart and his reverend colleagues at Andover, publicly thank Mr. Webster for recalling them to this sacred duty, which in their backslidden state they had almost forgotten? Why should Mr. Webster be ashamed of recommending the most efficient measures, for effecting the duty? or Mr. Stuart, be compelled to put language to the torture, to prove that Mr. Webster did *not* say, what it is plain he *did* say, and *ought* to have said, on his principles? Or does it prove that both of them are ashamed of the dirty and diabolical business of slave catching, after they have proved it right?

MR. STUART LOOKING SOUTH.

Space forbids me to follow Mr. Stuart's argument any farther. The remainder of his book is occupied with a curious mass of incoherencies, at which one might smile, if the spectacle of such a mind, doing such work, did not incline one to pity. He has an argument against the Wilmot proviso, spiteful enough to satisfy Mr. Calhoun: and weak enough to gratify the friends of freedom. But so ardent an admirer of Mr. Webster must of course, give a kick to a measure, which his lion master had killed. He belabors abolitionists with a heartiness, with an amount of misrepresentation which amply prove that his age and his habits, have not impaired his power to hate.

His closing address to slave-holders is worth reading. He becomes very respectful and affectionate, like one who is conscious of approaching a very august personage. With his hat in his hand, he reverently begins, "I am now going to say something to my respected fellow-citizens of the South." He then offers up the usual incense to South Carolina, declaring, "that in no state is there more gentlemanly comity and courtesy, and more high-souled chivalry; or a larger number of true and warm hearted Christians: that he has seen and conversed with many a kind hearted, moral, high minded Southerner." While piling up these sweet epithets on them, he is equally liberal of such affectionate words as these towards anti-slavery men:—"abolition diatribes"—"fanatics of the north"—"slander, contumely and vituperation"—"pestiferous howlings"—compares them to "Dominic, Jeffries, Loyola, Hindoo infanticides, naked Quakers," and all such lovely characters. Of the noble hearted GIDDINGS he says, "he should be sent to an insane hospital where he properly belongs."

One need add no comment to such developments of Northern servility: to baseness getting on its knees before pride and sin.

CONTRADICTIONS.

This singular book terminates with the author's views of slavery. They are of just the same value, as the stereotyped assertion with which every sturdy defender of the slaveholder always closes his argument; "but I hate slavery as bad as any body." It is no more than just however to give Mr. Stuart the benefit of his own contradictions, and we will place side by side a few of his original and profound opinions.

God "gives them express liberty to do this. Lev. 25: 44. [hold slaves] p. 11. "Slaves, which heaven has given express leave to purchase." p. 35.	"Slavery is a glaring contradiction of the first and fundamental principle of the Bible."

God, of course, gives men *express leave* to violate the first and fundamental principle of the Bible.

"the slave catcher—a man who can engage in that business is capable of *forging* any proof."	"Paul sent back a slave"—Of course, he "catched him" first. The law to send back fugitives "must be obeyed."

If it is a "duty" to send them back, it is a duty to catch them. But the man, bad enough to catch them, is bad enough to commit forgery.

"Talk of conscience in violating a solemn compact!" such a conscience is held up to scorn—page after page.	Of a law forbidding slaves to read he says, "Obedience to [such] human law is a *crime;* treason against the majesty of heaven and earth."
"Slaves are forbidden, 1 Cor. 7: 20, to be fractious, querulous, and *uneasy* MERELY because they are in bondage."	"the mass of slaves must and do live in a virtual state of concubinage." "Ignorance profound and universal is the *inevitable* lot of the great mass of all who are held in bondage." "The inevitable consequence is that females, ignorant and without a sense of delicacy, are at the mercy of their masters." "Slavery in its *best attitude*, even among Christian masters, is a degradation of a whole class."

The Bible "forbids men to be *uneasy*, MERELY because" they are in *such* a condition. Pages might be filled with similar beauties, and Mr. Stuart on the ground of such contradictions will probably deny that he can be charged with defending slavery.

But I have done. If any one after reading these pages should censure me for having treated great and venerable men with disrespect; my reply is, men of talent and learning, when they will consecrate their talent to the cause of truth and righteousness, I revere; nay I almost worship them as the true vice-gerents of God on earth. But if great men, prostitute their talents to the purposes of error, injustice and sin, if they voluntarily harness themselves up to drag the polluted gods of vice and slavery: then I cease to respect them: they ought to have no respect. If their greatness gives countenance to the wrong, and is planted as a bulwark for its defence, then are we bound to get at the sin, through or over the great men who have yoked themselves to such a service.

But as to the matters discussed in Mr. Stuart's book. any man of common sense is equally competent with these men who are termed great, to form an opinion. Indeed there are few men so unfit as Mr. Webster to decide questions of right and wrong. One hardly knows whether to feel indignation or contempt, when *such* a man gravely lectures us on our *duties!* attempts to enlighten our consciences! One would as soon receive Satan as an instructor in moral obligation because he is old and great.

The passages of Scripture on which Mr. Stuart expends so much elaborate trifling, are among the plainest and simplest in the Bible. If any plain, honest mind, is competent to form an opinion on any part of the word of God, he is able to form a just and decided opinion on these texts. One needs no giant intellect, no profound knowledge of Greek or Hebrew, to understand Paul when he tell us that he did NOT send back Onesimus as a servant: or to know the mind of God when he curses oppression.

Sad indeed is the sight when *such* men, employ themselves in *such* a work; the encouragement of slave catching. Gladly would one if duty allowed draw a covering over them as Noah's sons did over their fallen and disgraced father, and say

Oh, dumb be passions stormy rage
When he who might
Have lighted up, and led his age
Falls back in night.

*** Some typographical errors were overlooked by the proof reader, when the foregoing pages were struck off. In the following words, an error occurs as printed: polygamist—Procrustes—hermeneutics—Jeffries—grievously—pharisaically—&c. &c.

www.ingramcontent.com/pod-product-compliance
Lightning Source LLC
LaVergne TN
LVHW011139110826
845150LV00008B/2405

* 9 7 8 1 4 1 8 1 9 3 3 5 5 *